D1266321

Secrets of
LEADERSHIP

J. Donald Walters

Hardbound edition, first printing 1993

Text Illustrations: Karen White

ISBN 1-56589-034-5

10 9 8 7 6 5 4 3 2 1

PRINTED IN HONG KONG

Crystal Clarity
P U B L I S H E R S

14618 Tyler Foote Road, Nevada City, CA 95959
1 (800) 424-1055

A seed thought is offered for every day of the month. Begin a day at the appropriate date. Repeat the saying several times: first out loud, then softly, then in a whisper, and then only mentally. With each repetition, allow the words to become absorbed ever more deeply into your subconscious. Thus, gradually, you will acquire as complete an understanding as one might gain from a year's course in the subject. At this point, indeed, the truths set forth here will have become your own.

Keep the book open at the pertinent page throughout the day. Refer to it occasionally during moments of leisure. Relate the saying as often as possible to real situations in your life.

Then at night, before you go to bed, repeat the thought several times more. While falling asleep, carry the words into your subconscious, absorbing their positive influence into your whole being. Let it become thereby an integral part of your normal consciousness.

DAY 1

L

The Secret of
LEADERSHIP is...

to think of your position as an

opportunity to serve, not as a

trumpet call to self-importance.

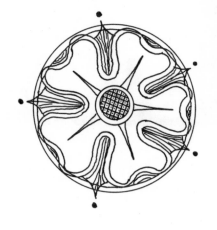

DAY 2

The Secret of **LEADERSHIP** is...

to hold always to the principle,
"People are more important
than things."

L

DAY 3

The Secret of **LEADERSHIP** *is...*

giving loyalty to those under you,

and not demanding it first of them.

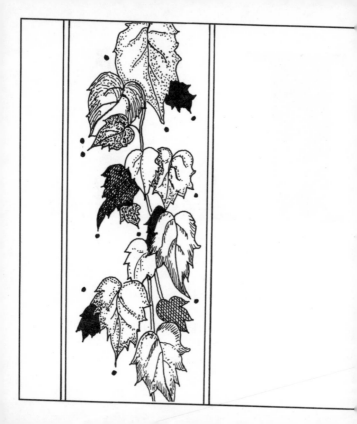

DAY 4

L

The Secret of LEADERSHIP is...

sharing the credit, but sharing with others their blame.

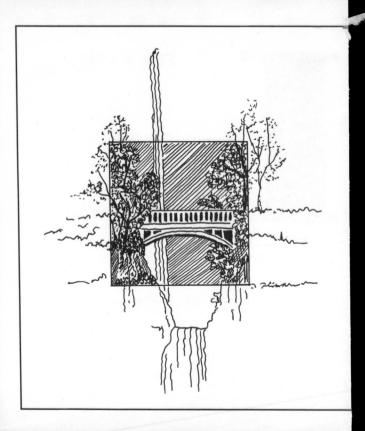

L

The Secret of
LEADERSHIP *is...*

allegiance to truth. Remember, truth

alone wins in the end.

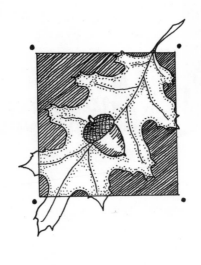

L DAY 6

The Secret of LEADERSHIP is...

bearing the larger picture always in mind. Ask yourself, "What are we *really* trying to accomplish?"

L DAY 7

The Secret of LEADERSHIP is...

even-mindedness: not being elated by success, nor depressed by failure, but simply doing your best, and letting the results take care of themselves.

DAY 8

L

The Secret of
EADERSHIP *is...*

to concentrate on what you are
doing, not on yourself as the doer.

DAY 9

L
The Secret of
LEADERSHIP is...

never to ask of others what you

would not willingly do yourself.

DAY 10

L

The Secret of **LEADERSHIP** *is...*

being impersonal where your own
well-being is concerned, but
personally concerned for the
well-being of others.

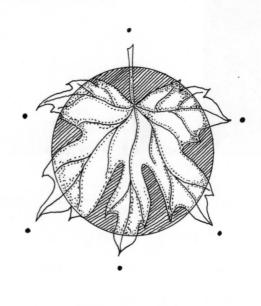

L

The Secret of
EADERSHIP *is...*

listening for the voice of reason in
others. Listening to what is really
trying to happen in every situation.

DAY 12

The Secret of LEADERSHIP is...

working with things as they are, not as you wish they were, nor as you think they ought to be: for the "impossible" dream can be attained only in *possible* stages.

DAY 13

L *The Secret of* **EADERSHIP** *is...*

working with others' abilities as
they are: not as you wish they were,
nor as you think they ought to be.

DAY 14

L

The Secret of **LEADERSHIP** *is...*

far-sightedness: gazing beyond

the visible to the potential

on the horizon.

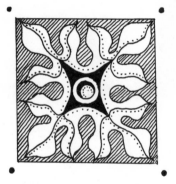

L

The Secret of
LEADERSHIP *is...*

to be solution-oriented,

not problem-oriented.

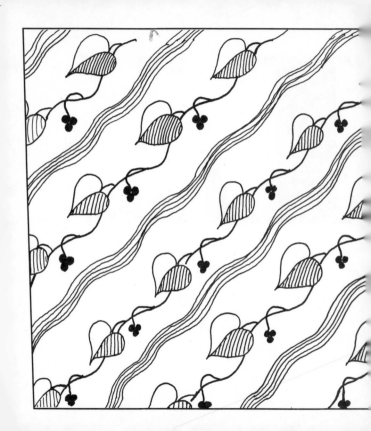

DAY 16

The Secret of
LEADERSHIP *is...*

not shackling yourself with what is
merely customary; on the other
hand, not confusing merit with
novelty. Do what is intrinsically
right, and, even if others have done
it a thousand times, it will seem new.

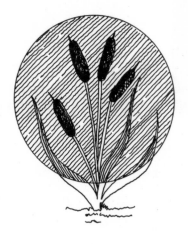

L

The Secret of
EADERSHIP *is...*

sharing with others your goals and
ideals. Include them as friends, and
you will have their support.

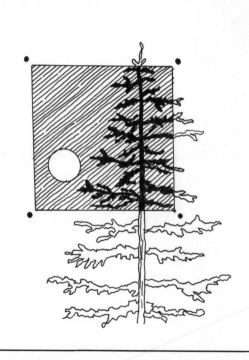

DAY 18

The Secret of LEADERSHIP is...

appealing to high principles, and
not seeking support by an appeal
to people's prejudices.

L

The Secret of
LEADERSHIP *is...*

recognizing in kindness and

compassion higher principles

than can be found in rules

and precedents.

DAY 20

L

The Secret of
LEADERSHIP *is...*

to consider the team more important
than the product. Remember, a good
team can develop many products.

DAY 21

L

The Secret of
LEADERSHIP *is...*

not allowing your decisions to

be influenced by personal

likes and dislikes.

L DAY 22

The Secret of LEADERSHIP is...

inviting cooperation from others,

rather than demanding

their obedience.

DAY 23

L *The Secret of* **EADERSHIP** *is...*

enthusiasm: winning others to your
ideas by the joy you yourself
feel in them.

L

The Secret of
LEADERSHIP is...

doing willingly whatever needs

to be done.

DAY 25

L

The Secret of
LEADERSHIP *is...*

finding joy in the doing, rather than
in the things done. Thereby, though
things change, your ability to inspire
others will remain constant.

DAY 26

The Secret of LEADERSHIP is...

to view whatever you do as a path to some greater good.

DAY 27

L

The Secret of LEADERSHIP is...

the ability to inspire others with faith in their own high potential.

DAY 28

L

The Secret of
LEADERSHIP *is...*

putting your heart in your work, and
not merely giving the work your
reasoned endorsement.

DAY 29

L
The Secret of
LEADERSHIP *is...*

loving others—not as separate from
yourself, but as part of your own
greater reality.

L

The Secret of
LEADERSHIP *is...*

magnanimity; not bearing grudges.

Remember, when people hurt you,

that they are hurting themselves

even more. Give them your

silent sympathy.

DAY 31

The Secret of LEADERSHIP is...

a sense of humor; laughing *with*
others, never *at* them.

Other Books in the **Secrets** Series
by J. Donald Walters

Secrets of Happiness

Secrets of Friendship

Secrets of Inner Peace

Secrets of Success

Secrets for Men

Secrets for Women

Secrets of Prosperity

Secrets of Self-Acceptance

Secrets of Winning People

Secrets of Radiant Health and Well-Being

Secrets of Bringing Peace on Earth

Selected Other Titles
by J. Donald Walters

The Art of Supportive Leadership
(book, audio, video)

How to Spiritualize Your Marriage

Education for Life

Money Magnetism

The Path (the autobiography of J. Donald Walters)

If you cannot find these books at your local gift or bookstore, write or call: Crystal Clarity, Publishers, 14618 Tyler Foote Road, Nevada City, CA 95959, or call 1-800-424-1055.

Design: Sara Cryer
Illustrations: Karen White
Typesetting: Robert Froelick
Photography: Mark McGinnis